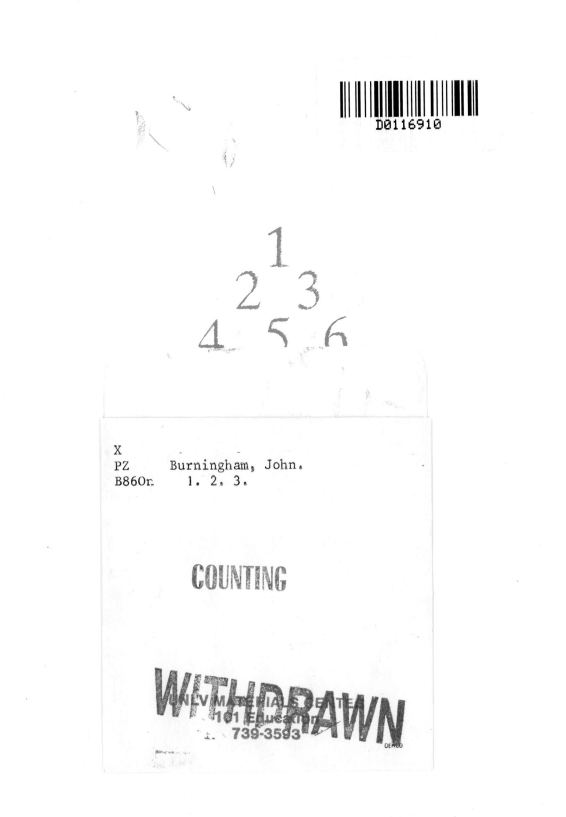

Originally published in Great Britain by
Walker Books, Ltd., 184–192 Drummond Street, London NW1 3HP
Published in the United States in 1986 by Crown Publishers, Inc.,
225 Park Avenue South, New York, New York 10003
CROWN is a trademark of Crown Publishers, Inc.
IT'S GREAT TO LEARN!   and logo
are trademarks of Crown Publishers, Inc.
Manufactured in Italy

Library of Congress Cataloging in Publication Data
Burningham, John.   John Burningham's 1 2 3.
Summary: A counting book that follows ten children
as they clamber up into a big tree, until they are
surprised by a final climber.
1. Counting—Juvenile literature. [1. Counting]
I. Title.   II. Title; 1 2 3.   III. Title: One, two, three.
IV. Title; John Burningham's one, two, three.
QA113.B88 1985 513'.2 [E] 85-13212
ISBN 0-517-55962-5
10 9 8 7 6 5 4 3 2 1
First American Edition

John Burningham's

123

CROWN PUBLISHERS, INC.   NEW YORK

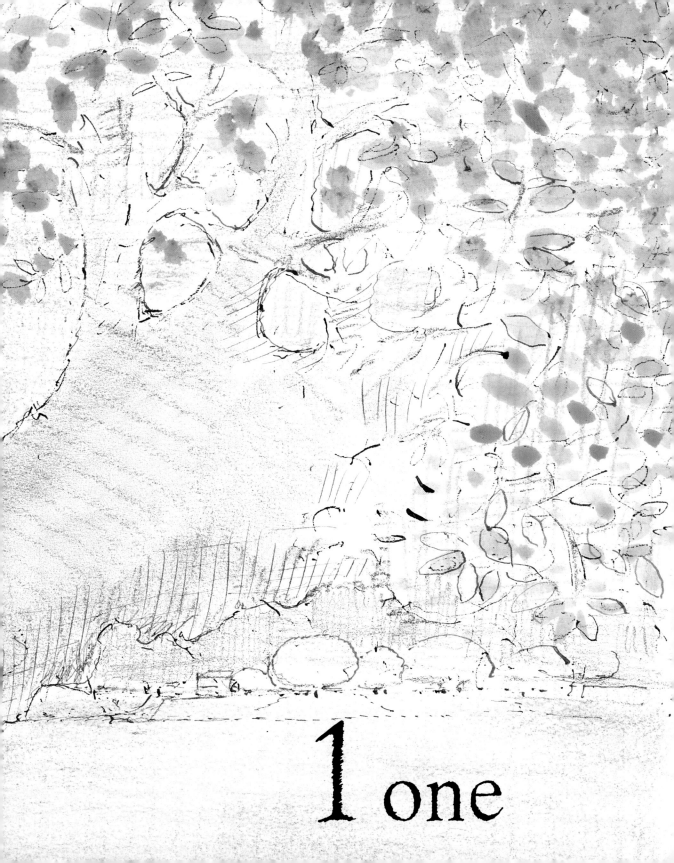

1 one

2 two

3 three

4 four

5 five

6 six

7 seven

8 eight

9 nine

10 ten